Latrece Johnson, M.Ed.

WHAT IS A PENINSULA?

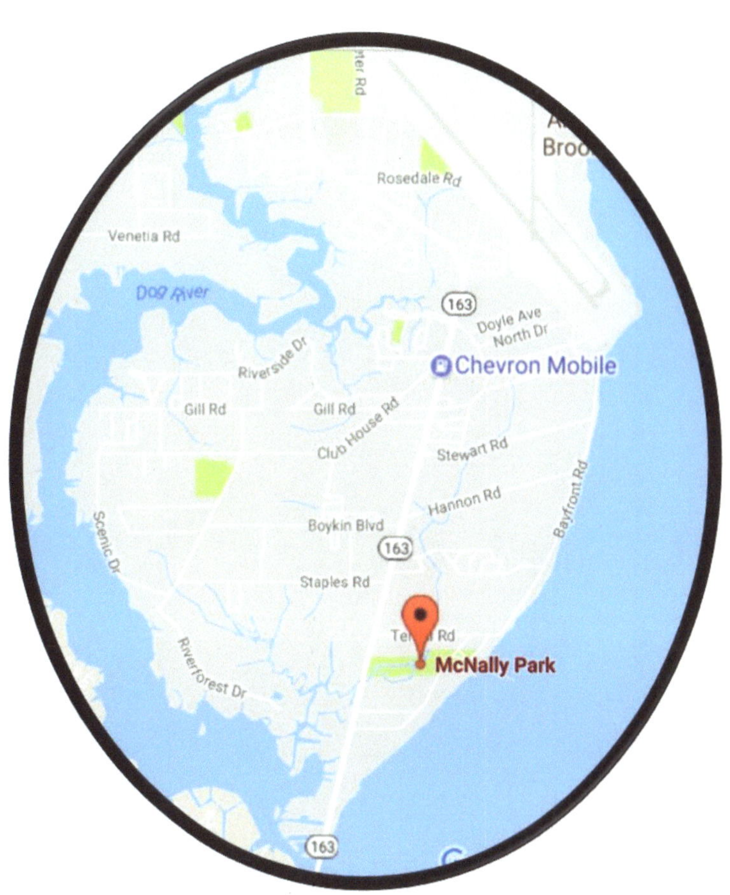

"Local Science by A Local Scientist" series

JOHNSON / Peninsula / 2

Dedicated to all who live on and love our waters.

--LJ

What is a

peninsula?

peninsula

pen·in·su·la
/pəˈninsələ/ 🔊

noun

a piece of land almost surrounded by water or projecting out into a body of water.
synonyms: cape, promontory, point, head, headland, foreland, ness, horn, bill, bluff
"residents on the peninsula take these storm warnings very seriously"

Peninsulas are pieces of land surrounded by water on three of its sides.

Other names for peninsulas include…

headlands, capes, islands, promontories, bills, points, or spits.

We live on a peninsula.

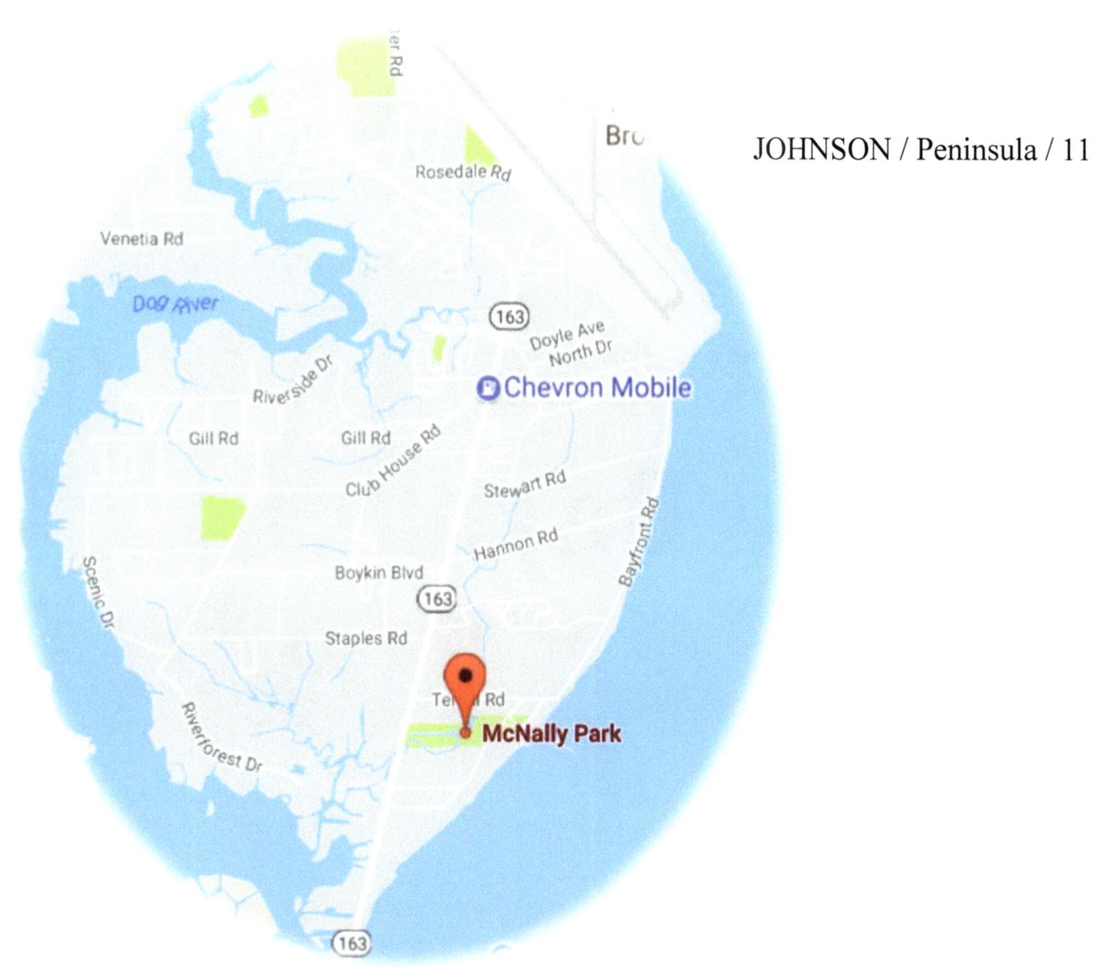
Rosedale Rd
Venetia Rd
Dog River
163
Doyle Ave
North Dr
Riverside Dr
Chevron Mobile
Gill Rd
Gill Rd
Club House Rd
Stewart Rd
Hannon Rd
Scenic Dr
Boykin Blvd
163
Staples Rd
Terrell Rd
McNally Park
Riverforest Dr
163
Bro

It is the Peninsula of Mobile Bay.

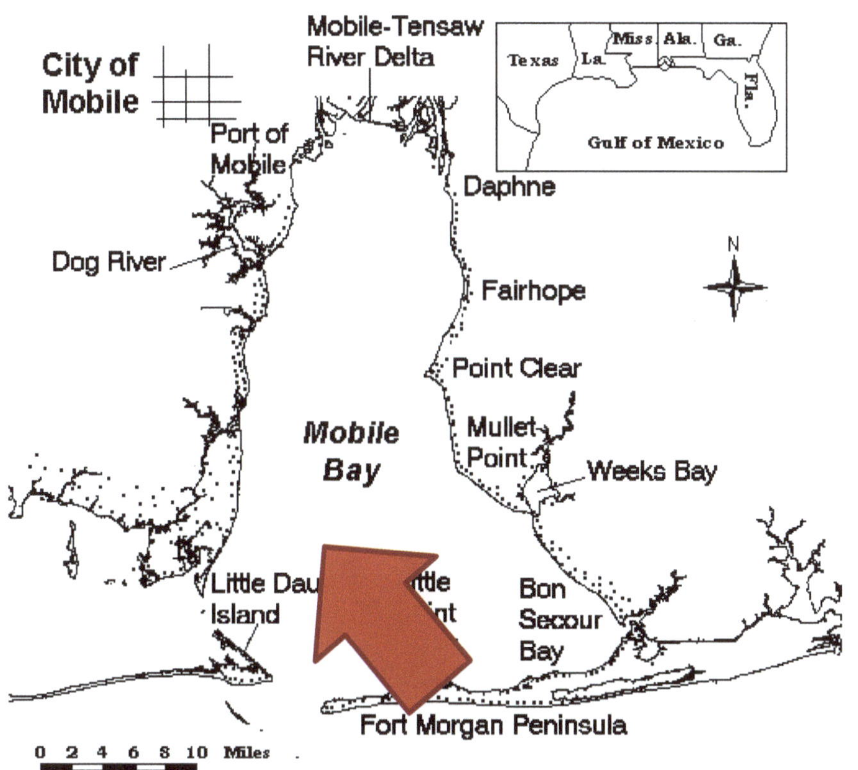

Gulf of Mexico

Located along Dauphin Island Parkway (Hwy 163), the peninsula is…

Sigler Ave
Sigler Ave
Dauphin Island Pkwy
Hannon Rd
H
Skinner Service
ley
ool
Boykin Blvd
Google

bounded on the north by Interstate 10, …

WEST
EAST
INTERSTATE
INTERSTATE
10
10

on the south and west by Dog River…

AL
Mobile
Gulf of Mexico
Legend
Hydrography
Interstates
Waterways
Miles
0   5   10
I-65
I-10
Dog River
Mobile Bay

and on the east by Mobile Bay.

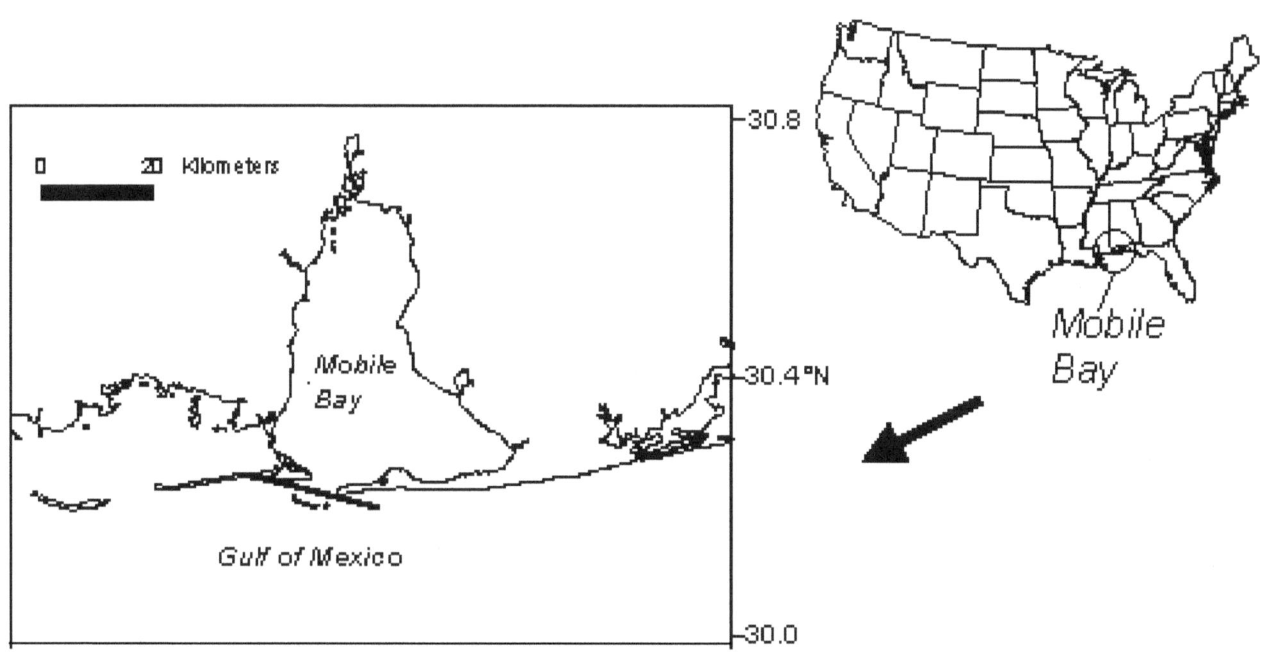
0   20   Kilometers
Mobile
Bay
Gulf of Mexico
30.8
30.4°N
30.0
Mobile
Bay

The Peninsula of Mobile Bay is five miles long, three miles wide at its widest point. It is home to a diverse community of over 11,000 people.

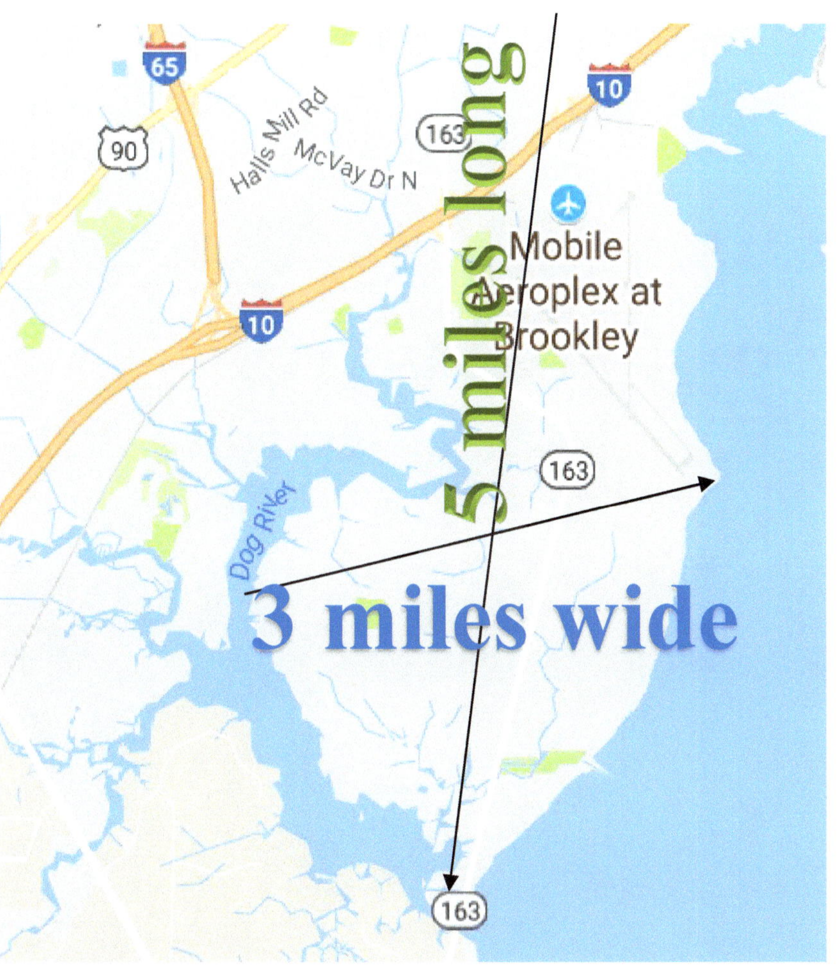
65
90
163
Halls Mill Rd
McVay Dr N
10
Mobile Aeroplex at Brookley
5 miles long
Dog River
163
3 miles wide
163

The **Peninsula** is Mobile's gateway to nature.

The wetlands and waterways provide habitat for a diverse population of wildlife and marine life such as alligators, eagles, manatees, and turtles.

The **peninsula** offers recreational opportunities like fishing, powerboating, sailing, canoeing, kayaking, birdwatching, and cycling.

How do you enjoy life on the peninsula?

Questions for Comprehension

1. What is a **peninsula**?
2. Give the name of the **peninsula** you learned about in this book.
3. What type of animals live on a **peninsula**?
4. What kinds of activities can you do on a **peninsula**?

Peninsula Math and Science

With paper and pencil, draw a large map of the Peninsula of Mobile Bay. Use your favorite blocks or building materials to model its length and width.

Video Information about Peninsulas

Difference between island and peninsula.
https://www.youtube.com/watch?v=14EilCea4YM

Holy Family Academy. Island, Peninsula, Isthmus Review.
https://www.youtube.com/watch?v=1UNaeNmjHU8

The GeoScholar. Geography - Landforms: Peninsulas.
https://www.youtube.com/watch?v=1CwTI_Qbgz8